AWAKENED

A Peaceful Revolution

Self-Published by Rob Bartlett

Awakened

Copyright 2019 by Rob Bartlett

Self-Published with Create Space by Rob Bartlett

www.wizardawakened.com

ISBN-13: 978-0-578-57356-4

DEDICATED TO THE
EARTH'S HEALING

Lift your gaze to the rise

Of new generations.

Like arrows they soar

Toward Aquarian's Dawn.

Muted voices no longer

These young Dreamers fly

Unfettered and bold

On currents connected.

Arouse, fragile earth!

Heed each healing whisper

For your steadfast guardians

Were born to awaken us,

A peaceful revolution is near.

Lynne Barstow

ACKNOWLEDGMENTS

I first acknowledge my captive audience of many customers, friends, and acquaintances who had to listen to my new theories and inspirations with the usual response of, "It really is nice to hear something positive." After hearing this for a while I began to realize there is a book here and hence my inspiration.

I thank Jean Dunham for the first editorial run through for her great ideas and influence. Thanks to my close friend, Louise Warnock who is always available to bounce ideas off her enlightened, conscious mind. Special thanks go to Lexie Smith Sinatra and Audrey Brandolino, both Gen Z friends, for their input and suggestions which I listened to.

Special thanks go to my good friend David Turner who read the manuscript three times for editing purposes. His best friend, Kelly Cramer, did an even more thorough job of editing. If there are any mistakes, it is their faults.

My graphic artist friend, Matthew Baker was a dream to work with. He has been responsible for the design and manifestation of my vision for the book cover. It has become a family tradition for my niece to write a dedication poem for each one of my books. I am in awe of her abilities and talents.

Contents

INTRODUCTION

In this book I am recognizing these newer generations as the people who will save our planet. Through my observation, conversations, and futurist thinking, I see that a social and consciousness revolution is underway. Please keep in mind that I must speak in generalities because there are always exceptions to every rule.

One of my endeavors is to give some background on these newer generations and where they are coming from. Understanding and gaining respect for these youths is my ultimate goal. I also desire to help these younger people understand and energize the potential power they can yield to better the planet.

First, the Baby Boomers made the break from old rigid thinking by getting out of their heads. Each generation since, has taken this process to higher levels of open heart with major implications.

Each generation appears to be evolving away from structured thinking while aligning more and more with their hearts. Heart must be the power and spiritual connection to save the planet.

These generations will right the wrongs of centuries-old patriarchal controls of ego, power, and greed.

There also appears to be some possible parallels to Biblical prophecy. These basic truths suggest these young people could be the carriers of a God-ordained salvation.

The use of the word God in this book is to be interpreted on a personal level in the reader's own understanding. God is referred to in many ways, such as a strong connection with a force or power in the universe beyond ourselves. God can be referenced as Spirit, All In One, The Force, Higher Power, The Source, Great Mystery, The Greater Parent, etc.

CHAPTER 1

Background

A mystery is afoot. A subtle social change is happening amongst the new generations. Pundits and authorities know something is different, but they are not quite sure what it is or what it represents. Could this be a harbinger of something unique? Could this also be a renaissance of social evolvement?

We Baby Boomers were the beginning of the shift. Throughout history, children were to be seen but not heard. The pendulum of social morals had swung in both directions throughout changing times, but the one constant had always remained, children were not to be heard.

Baby Boomers effected the change. It is possible to come up with dozens of reasons for this change. Could it be the mass-information age, the latch-key generation bringing both parents into the work force, influenced further by the end of WWII? Were parents distracted and/or relieved with the end of war and having more mobility and money? Were parents feeling more connected to their children? Could it have been that Maslow's Hierarchy of Needs was being met?

I feel it's bigger than all these issues put together. What single force could be greater than and influence a multitude of small changes to create a major change? This cannot be an accident or a chance happening. It had to be a power greater than anything else, the power of God or of higher creation.

Historically, social structure had been fairly rigid with lots of judgments. This would include right and wrong, good and bad, should and shouldn't, do's and don'ts, compiled with prejudice. These are all structured thinking patterns and taught belief systems.

As a child during the 1950's, I remember many restrictions and judgments. I was raised to believe the most important life achievements represented getting an advanced education, getting married, and raising children. Respectful couples got married before living together and having sex. A woman who went into a bar by herself was considered a slut. The movies at that time never showed a couple sharing the same bed; they had twin beds. My parents suggested that the children from interracial marriages would always be outcasts. I always tried to point out that that kind of thinking is what created the problem, but to no avail.

When a child is raised with less structure, the mind or thinking (judgement) process is lessened or diminished and is replaced with developing intuition, heart, and feelings. The Baby Boomers were the first generation to evolve into less structure and began to feel things no other group ever had. The counter cultures of the 1960's were some of the first manifestations.

These young adults began to act out from feelings of hurt, pain, shame, and restrictions from previous generations. They began demanding more social justice and loosened rules. Alternative lifestyles erupted into hippies, flower children, beatniks, etc. Communes became popular, allowing for freer relationships and lifestyles. Many felt a need for a different form of community.

The Baby Boomer generation raised their children with less structure; the less the structure, the more the feelings. Each subsequent generation has been raised with even less structure. Of course, there are always exceptions to these generalities. But from a broader perspective, a more feeling, compassionate, sympathetic, populace is becoming the norm.

As the Baby Boomers first explored their awakening feelings, there was not a well-defined direction or purpose. They knew something was not right with the structure of society and war. This was the beginning of a rebellion against restrictions and judgements, exhibited through demonstrations, drugs, and free

sex. The revolution had begun.

CHAPTER 2

The New Generation

These new generations are distinguished by titles such as Millennials, Gen X, Gen Y and Gen Z. Their characteristics are somewhat different from previous generations. Generally speaking, they are the most heart-centered, intuitive, feeling group on the planet today.

These youth are generally less materialistic, but they do like their electronics. They tend to group date and hang out, as opposed to individual dating. They are not in a hurry to drive, get married, or have children. They have little racial prejudice, hence more interracial relationships.

We Baby Boomers had more ego as we were making the transition from head to heart. These young people are so much further into their hearts that there is little room for ego which would otherwise be cultivated by intellect or head.

A strong sense of community is important to this group of feelers. Through heart they feel a need for stronger connections to their fellow mankind. Compassion and empathy are fostered and nourished as they thrive in this environment. Non-feelers or head-centered people can be loners or maintain fewer people connections.

Because feelers possess more intense connection to heart, they have more consciousness and are more compassionate about their beliefs and purposes. These youth, for the most part, believe in God or a higher power but shun the restrictions of religion. Their spirituality is of a more internal experience rather than a belief system, centered in the heart rather than the head. They have much more wisdom which is developed by combining heart and experience. I define wisdom as knowledge tempered by heart.

I frequently meet teenagers who have become vegetarians for the main reason they don't want animals killed for their food. Others want a plant-based diet for environmental reasons. Their commitment is very strong. I never had any conviction at that age to be vegan. Today I have cut back my meat eating habits dramatically, but I am not ready to completely give it up. My generation were historically big meat eaters.

As juvenile Baby Boomers, most of us had a small circle of friends, a half dozen or fewer. With technology, these new generations often are communicating with as many as 40-50 friends. This is an incredibly expanded world. Their influences and exposures are coming from all directions.

Older generations often express their thoughts that these kids don't know how to communicate because they text rather than talk. I don't agree with that. They communicate more than ever, just in alternate ways. I speak with many youths in my line of work and find the exchange to be most gratifying. I find many of these teenagers to have a wisdom and directness beyond levels that I had at that age. They can be shockingly honest. I also find their social graces to be just fine. Of particular interest, they take pride in being nerds, which my generation was hostile to. I love the changes.

Music has always been a form of expression for each generation and these young people have expressed their protest in music such as hip hop and rap. This form of rebellion is worldwide. Powerful messages can be conveyed this way as a tool against totalitarian regimes. Russia arrested two members of the band Pussy Riot and incarcerated them for two years.

Every new generation is becoming better informed than the last with expanding technology. These youth are being exposed to more and more knowledge, making it the most well-informed generation ever. Compounded with heart, these people have developed a greater wisdom.

These younger generations have different work values. We Baby Boomers were raised with a strong Judeo-Christian work ethic. Our hard-working parents expected their children to become hard-working adults. If you changed jobs very often you could be considered unstable. Loyalty and dedication were highly respected.

In retrospect, many Baby Boomers have expressed sadness for a loss of quality family time in exchange for their dedicated work ethic. Maybe these new heart-centered generations will make more quality time for their spouses and children.

This new generation puts "feel good" and the "pursuit of happiness" above the pressures of social expectations. Loyalty to work and the company is no longer a priority. It's more important to be satisfied with one's work, feel that the work contributes to the greater good, and feel fulfilled. One of my young friends said to me, "We work to live, we don't live to work."

I have read that many of the latest generation hold solidly to a personal standard that began with the Baby Boomers to not work for defense contractors and the military. They have also demanded better treatment for women and minorities. In April 2019, Amazon workers enacted the largest employee driven movement on climate change in the tech industry in order to reduce its carbon footprint. Google employees are making similar changes.

An article by Ellie Silverman in the Philadelphia Inquirer (information taken from a recent Morning Consult study conducted in May 2019) states that Gen Z still prefers shopping in stores. In her analysis of the study, Ellie Silverman reveals that, "Gen Z is on track to be the largest, most ethnically diverse, best-educated, and most financially powerful generation ever." Then the report states, "In the coming years, their distinctive habits will play an outsized role in shaping American culture and commerce." These younger adults appear to find value in supporting local businesses and the cottage industries.

Higher consciousness suggests that it is more important to "Be" rather than to

"Do." Is this another manifestation of social evolution? The ancient religions have a strong spiritual understanding of God connectedness. For example, Buddhism says it is more important to "Be" rather than to "Do." To "Do" is more aligned with Judeo-Christian work ethic. "Doing" is a masculine, dominant distraction, preoccupation, avoidance, and oriented to high production. To "Be" is a closer connection to God and Spirit. "Being" is a feminine, listening, receptive position. It is the, "means to an end," for spiritual connection and Godliness. I think these new generations are being affected by a newer, stronger alignment with God and Spirit, which explains the behavior changes, identifications, and thinking. They are less driven by ego and more connected to self-awareness and self-love.

Historically, large parts of the Midwest and southern United States have their own mentality. In these regions, people tend to function in large or extended family units. This is a form of tribalism. Tribal groups tend to have very insular thinking. Each generation is raised with the same values, judgments, and prejudices which are very limited, and contribute to a narrow, fixed, world view. Religion is a major influence on this restricted thinking.

However, technology will have a massive influence on this part of the country. This very available, expanded information is exposing these youth to broader and more flexible, progressive thinking. These younger children will no longer be as trapped in a limited consciousness and will begin to move beyond family, tribalistic fears, judgments, and prejudices. Families will no longer have the major influence they once had on their children. This will help bring insular communities into the mainstream.

CHAPTER 3

Social Change

Social changes are becoming apparent. These new heart-centered generations are expressing a need for more social justice and transparency in government and industry. The "#MeToo" movement and the increase in public whistleblowers are good examples of this. These issues, such as individual voice and personal boundaries have lain dormant for generations, but no longer.

These younger people have done more to save the planet and promote gun control in a short time compared to a paralyzed, immobilized older generation. These older, head-centered folks are controlled by fear, power, greed, and money from the establishment. Fear is a part of head function and denies access to heart. Young people functioning from heart have a minimal fear component.

An older head-centered person would look at the bottom line of a financial statement and think in terms of money. Is there a positive or negative cash flow which identifies a situation as successful or unsuccessful, good or bad? A monetary amount can be attached to any circumstance to give it a rating or value on which to make a decision.

The heart-centered feeler gives the bottom line a whole new definition, usually associated with the human race. Is a project of benefit or not to the population? The focus is no longer on the money but on how it improves human life. You would not be able to put a value on life or social benefits, even if not being cost effective.

Politically, this component is moving left. Heart-centered people are more focused on empathy, compassion, and social justice. These attitudes are more democratic and progressive. We have a very strong pro-socialistic (democratic socialism) attitude developing, moving into all fields including medicine and education.

Take California for example, where these attitudes are exemplified. There is a Democratic super majority in the state government. There is an old adage that says, "As California goes, so goes the nation." I'd like to add, "So goes the world."

California tends to be a trail blazer in social change cultivated by a more heart-centered, feeling population. Some make fun of these Californians. I see it as a trend toward compassion to provide the highest and greatest good for the greatest number in our ever-increasing interconnectedness on this planet.

On a national level the statistics support similar political changes. In 2018, voters under 30 supported Democratic House candidates by 67%. A 2018 Pew survey found that 59% of millennial voters identify as Democrats. Recent surveys of Generation Z voters (those born between 1997 and 2012) have found they are more liberal than Millennials.

Ronald Brownstein, in the *Atlantic*, pointed out that younger Democrats prefer a more progressive candidate who they think can bring systemic change as opposed to the older who focus on who can win.

It is estimated that within two decades America will be a majority minority country. Polls tell us that 79% of millennials think immigration is good for America and 61% think racial diversity is good for the country. Conservative thought seems to be getting less relevant to the America that is coming into being.

The statistics present a supportive picture of teens being more cautious, more tame, and more responsible. David Finkelhor, a sociology professor and director of the Crimes Against Children Research Center at the University of New Hampshire expresses, "In the long term, the trends are quite clear, but even the short term, we're undergoing a period of dramatic improvements that have not been widely acknowledged or underlined and it's too bad."

Overall, teenage adolescence is safer than it has ever been. Statistics show this new generation has fewer car accidents and fewer physical fights. Teenagers today are less likely to drop out of high school, less likely to have sex, less likely to get pregnant, and commit fewer crimes.

The Center for Disease Control and Prevention has many surveys which reveal behavior changes amongst our teenagers. Surprisingly enough, sex with multiple partners is falling. The percentage of high school juniors who have ever had sexual intercourse has declined to 42% from 62% since 1991.

The use of nearly every type of drug, including alcohol and tobacco, has been falling among teenagers for decades, according to a long-standing survey conducted by researchers at the University of Michigan. Hallucinogen use for 10th graders is down about a third from the 1990's. Alcohol use is down more than 40% from the 1990's. Cigarette use has fallen for 10th graders even more, from 30% down to 4%. The major exception is marijuana which is at the same level of a generation ago and is used by one in four of 10th graders.

The greatest problem for a new generation of sensitive, heart-centered feelers has resulted in an increased rate of suicide. The incidence of certain mental health diagnoses, mostly anxiety and depression likely from poor job opportunities and environmental issues, are becoming more common. From 2008 through 2014 the annual rate of suicide began increasing. Since 2014, the suicide rate has increased approximately 10% per year. The overall rate in 2017 was about twice that in 2000 based on available C.D.C. data.

An emotionally sensitive generation has used drugs as a form of suppression and denial. Head centered people have used socially acceptable means to suppress hurt, pain, and suffering like compulsive behavior. Compulsive work habits and hobbies have always been a great outlet. In a suppressed feeler, unrequited pain can turn into violence as externalized anger. Heart-centered people, on a healing path, must access their feelings to process them. Sensitive people can more easily work through their anxieties with therapy.

Drug use can also be recreational and used by these young people as a route to get closer to higher source. Hallucinogens are especially effective to open and accelerate the connections to the God within or the unconscious. Under proper guidance a vision quest can be very healing.

Emotionally troubled feelers also like to have community. A negative aspect of wanting to belong can lead to radical groups such as the neo-Nazis. The drive to belong can seduce these youth to some fairly dark places of hate and bigotry and are easily found online.

I always found it interesting to think back to my childhood when therapy was considered only for truly emotionally handicapped, non-functional people. Anyone who went to therapy in those days had to be very sick or "whacked out" and were looked down upon. Today with a more enlightened generation, therapy is considered the recognition of a need to achieve balance and well-being and is a "rite of passage."

Older generations had fewer career and social choices which likely kept life simpler. Often a son just followed in his father's footsteps. The new world has exploded with choices which can make life's decisions much more complicated and overwhelming. It can appear that these kids are floundering but because they are not as fear-based and more intuitive combined with faith, they coast through uncertainty with less apprehension. Again, I do not deny an increased probability of anxiety and depression, as their future can look questionable due to poor job outlook and environmental concerns. Hopefully they eventually find something that feels good.

Sexual identity is another fascinating aspect of these newer generations. Sexual fluidity has become quite common. A part of becoming more aware of one's feelings can turn into sexual exploration with fewer boundaries. Bisexuality and pansexuality have become much more common and acceptable. These youth don't have the judgments of older generations. Identifying as the opposite of their biological sex has led to more sexual reassignments.

Some of these young adults think of themselves as gender neutral or gender fluid. Therefore, I believe that on the higher spiritual plains we are non-sexual and androgynous. Are these people connecting themselves to a higher truth of non-identity? Assuming that God or Spirit is androgynous, why can't we move in that direction?

Are these youth rebelling or are they seeking deeper truths? Are they identifying with their soul as opposed to their mind or their body? The old standard is to be a man or woman and live within those parameters. However, the soul is boundless, and I believe these kids are exploring the extremities of what that might be.

A passage in the Bible refers to us becoming "One with God," (Corinthians 6:17). As these younger people become more closely aligned with their intuition and love, could they be moving closer to becoming one with God? They function the most strongly of any generation from their heart. Their passions and concerns are at the highest levels ever.

Another passage in the Bible says, "Only the children shall enter the kingdom of Heaven," (Matthew 18:3). You must define what a child is as not childish but childlike. I see them as a person of truth, trusting in their heart, non-judgmental, innocent, and not fear-based. I observe a lot of these young adults, both personally and in the news, whose demeanor is moving closer to these qualifications.

I feel that both Biblical prophecies might be being created right now on our Earth. Maybe it's not somewhere out there but instead happening right now, right here. With the evolution that these generations are creating, anything is possible. Heart is extremely powerful.

In the news we frequently read about the courage these children have when it comes to world issues. For example,

Melala Yousafzai from Pakistan received the Nobel Peace Prize after surviving a shooting for trying to insist on the availability of education for young girls. I read recently that in China the young kids were protesting, not over Communism, but for the lack of transparency in the government. The other problem in Hong Kong centers around the proposal to allow extraditions to mainland China. Newspaper reports reveal most demonstrators have been in their teens or twenties.   It's very difficult to take freedoms away from young feelers once they have had them.

Protecting the Earth and its environment has become the largest issue.   In Sweden, 16-year-old Greta Thunberg demonstrated outside the Swedish parliament for climate protection in late 2018. She has been nominated for a Nobel Peace Prize. She addressed the United Nations Climate Change Summit to say they were not doing enough to stop climate change.   She has been an inspiration for unified, youthful demonstrations worldwide for the same purpose.

These youth don't seem to be in a hurry to have children, and if so, not many. Many view that over population is by far the most significant problem we have on our planet. The strain on resources, therefore, water, farmland, and the oceans are nearing the breaking point. Moreover, religion has made no effort to address this issue, but encourage more babies. These generations understand the complexities of this problem for their future is at stake.

CHAPTER 4

Mass-Consciousness

I see a new component arising, a massive new concept. It is most easily illustrated by the example of a flock of birds or a school of fish that by the hundreds or thousands can turn on a dime in complete unison. Science is beginning to explore this mystery.

I see it as a phenomenon of mass-consciousness or of one-mindedness. These creatures are functioning as one or having one mind. Science suggests that we humans are more influenced by mass-consciousness than we realize or understand. A good example of this is the alleged experiment called the "Hundredth Monkey" which took place around the 1950's. This is not a human example but nevertheless illustrates the point of interconnectedness.

This experiment illustrated that as a learned behavior developed and spread to other associates, eventually critical mass was reached. In a flash, all members of the species picked up the identical behavior without previous knowledge or exposure to a set of actions. This can best be explained by mass-consciousness.

These new human generations are developing stronger heart and intuitive connections. This is not in the distant future. It is happening now. Heart and love are the most powerful energies available to humans. As these energies develop, grow, and connect, this mass-consciousness will be unstoppable.

These new generations are beginning to function as a unit. Truth, sympathy, and compassion will be the driving force to bring them together in a unified field. Goodness can be the only result because heart, love, and truth eliminate negative desires and outcomes.

Intellect or head function is our downfall because it rationalizes and justifies the ego. There is no uniformity in this energy, which has only self-interest in mind and can be destructive. This energy has little common ground or compromise which accounts for most of the problems in the world historically.

Heart is the advantage for the youth which is comprised of love, compassion, sympathy, forgiveness, and gratitude. It has one purpose and a common goal, which is to improve the human race.

This unifying gift or power will be most utilized by these new generations in two dominant areas, their voting and buying habits. Washington D.C. will never be the same again. These youth are beginning to see through the fake news, lies, propaganda, and falsehoods. They are recognizing integrity and truth in candidates. Only the good will prevail as they are not easily fooled. Their voting will change the world.

Likewise, this power block will be well utilized in their buying habits. Businesses that stay caught up in greed and power will ultimately disappear. Boycotting in mass will be their power tool. The toxic companies will be eliminated quickly. Those companies that are conscious and look out for the betterment of humanity will thrive. This will be a force to be reckoned with.

Starting around September/October 2019 a phenomenon started happening. On multiple continents, rebellions and protests began flaring up. The young people appear to be the catalyst. Ali Soufan, chief executive of The Southern Group, a security intelligence consultancy, has this to say, "It's young people who have had enough. This new generation are not buying into what they see as the corrupt order of the political and economic elite in their own countries. They want change."

In so many cases, little issues have turned into broader problems. The concerns are framed primarily around inequality, economic woes, and low faith in leaders. Could it be that these young people in these widely dispersed cultures and countries might be subtly connecting into a level of mass-consciousness? What better way to explain the recent sharp acceleration of protest worldwide.

As mentioned in chapter 3, a quote in the Bible says eventually we become "One with God." This is how I feel it will happen. As these younger become more intuitive and in their heart space, they will also be in their God space, representing and being one with God.

I believe this unity will be the force and power to unravel generations of destructive unconsciousness and heal the planet. A U. N. panel report by scientific world experts that was published in early 2019 issued an alarming projection of rapidly deteriorating, failing ecosystems caused by global warming. This deterioration will effect our economies, livelihoods, food security, health, and quality of life worldwide. An Australian report projects the end of life on this planet by the year 2050.

We can and will make the changes now. Success requires cooperation on a global scale. These newer generations will rise to the challenges through a unified awakened consciousness of heart. The momentum is rapidly building. We are moving worldwide into a heart-centered culture which I feel is the rudiments of the Heaven on Earth. I firmly believe this shift of consciousness, away from structure, is God's way of implementing a plan to save us from ourselves.

CHAPTER 5

Love and Creation

I write this chapter as a further illustration of the connection between love energy and ultimately to mass-consciousness.

I define love in terms of energy. Most people believe love is the most powerful energy in the universe. The divine definition of love is represented as feminine, passive, and motionless, but not lifeless. It represents all future potential waiting to be expressed.

The polar energy of love is light which is the divine masculine and the active. From inspiration comes manifestation. From the passive comes the active. From the passive feminine comes the active masculine.

It is necessary to have love and light in order to have life. You could consider this to be the fundamental trinity, the mother, the father, and the child. The mother is love, the father is light, and the child is life. Most religions have a trinity.

This energy concept can be moved or superimposed into the third dimension in our everyday world. What is the feminine energy that is passive, motionless, and waiting to be expressed? It can only be magnetic. There it sits waiting to be activated or released. A good example would be in a generator or a hydroelectric dam where the magnet is rotating around electric coils. This action creates electricity and is the male energy. From this passive female energy comes the active male energy. This action creates polarity which creates movement. Everything is in constant movement. The Native Americans, the Lakota, speak of "taku wakan skan skan," Sacred energy is always in motion.

When you combine electric energy and magnetic energy, you create electromagnetic energy which is the foundation of creation. All physical matter is electromagnetic energy. All creation falls somewhere on the spectrum, from high frequency radio waves to the lowest frequency or vibration comprising dense matter.

All energy retains memory which, in totality, becomes consciousness, out of which comes intelligence. As an example of how matter holds memory, I have seen a psychic pick up a piece of jewelry and describe its owner accurately. All electromagnetic energy, including matter, has a level of consciousness, some forms higher than others. Human souls have the highest levels and we are the most highly individuated, out of which comes intelligence. Lower life forms have a mass awareness. All memory is consciousness and is how we all connect. The highest frequencies of electromagnetic energy represent the greater creative force. Some people call this "The Force." We are all ultimately one! A common thought is "God is everything and everywhere."

Love is the basis and the origin of "The Force." Love is the original energy of the universe and that is why we hear the message that "Love is all there is." We were created in Love.

Because of duality we easily become injured and separated from our emotional bodies. Duality portrays us as being created in negative and positive, light and love thus making choices therein. The active left brain (where ego exists) represents the powerful, destructive, nonfeeling aspect, versus the passive right-brain. Adam and Eve are symbolic of this separation or temptation. When the ego is not balanced with heart, it can be willful and destructive. We make mistakes and then spend the rest of our lives trying to heal and reconnect with self-love.

If we were created in God's image, what would that look like? In my estimation I see it as a left-brain, right-brain concept; the left-brain is active light, the right-brain is intuitive love. God is both love and light. I do not see God as a physical form. Each one of us is an aspect of God in our brain, it being both active and passive, love and light.

The old adage that we only use 10% of our brain easily fits into this paradigm. The active left-brain dominates the passive 90% of the right-brain.

Meditation is the most effective route to access the 90% of the intuitive brain. By quieting the brain, God communicates with us through intuition and heart.

Most, if not all, religions practice a form of prayer which is a form of meditation. By stilling the mind we access intuition and heart. By understanding the workings of the God within, we are better able to access a direct channel to the higher being.

We easily get lost or injured through judgment, prejudice, hate, fear, emotional, physical, and sexual abuse, or abandonment issues. Freud claimed the formative years, 1-6, was when the most emotional damage occurred. We then can spend the rest of our lives trying to heal and forgive ourselves of fear, guilt, shame, and self-judgment.

The beauty of these new generations is their willingness to be more heart-centered, open and honest, therefore not suppressing their emotional injuries and becoming more willing to heal. Each newer generation is going further and getting better on the healing spectrum. This is a major part of what the "Human Experience" is all about. More of these people have a healthier relationship with love and its benefits of strength, confidence, and good intentions. Love is all there is and the end all, not the concept, but the embracing and integrating of it into one's everyday actions and feelings. This is the power of LOVE.

Awakened